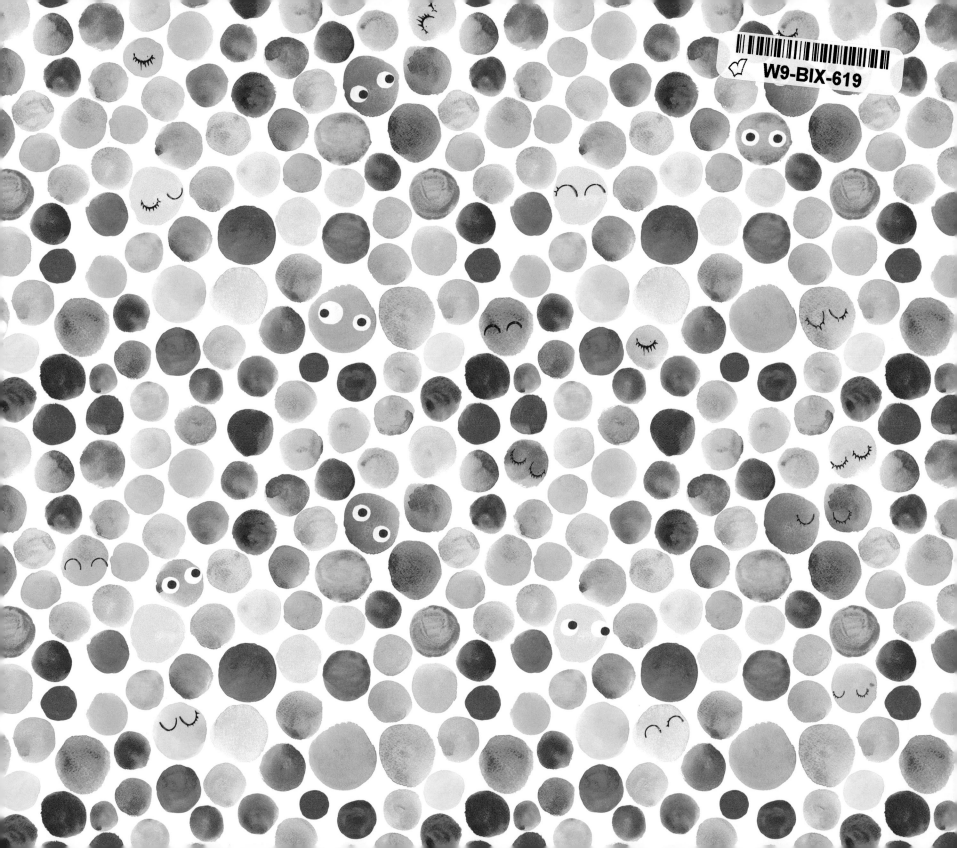

TO MISHA,
THE GARDNER,
AND ZENO,
THE SPROUT

Special thanks to Klaudyna Borewicz, PhD (microbiota researcher), for reviewing the text

Millbrook Press™
An imprint of Lerner Publishing Group, Inc.
241 First Avenue North
Minneapolis, MN 55401 USA

For reading levels and more information, look up this title at www.lernerbooks.com.

Designed by Lindsey Owens.
Main body text set in Avenir LT Pro. Typeface provided by Linotype.
The illustrations in this book were created with watercolor and some digital wizardry.

Library of Congress Cataloging-in-Publication Data

Names: D'yans, Masha, author, illustrator.
Title: A garden in your belly : meet the microbes in your gut / Masha D'yans.
Description: Minneapolis : Millbrook Press, 2020. | Audience: Ages 7–11 | Audience: Grades 2–3 | Summary: "Your belly is full of tiny creatures! Vivid watercolors and lively text teach kids about the garden of microscopic flora growing inside them, how it keeps them healthy, and how they can help it thrive" —Provided by publisher.
Identifiers: LCCN 2019049985 (print) | LCCN 2019049986 (ebook) | ISBN 9781541578401 (library binding) | ISBN 9781728401454 (ebook)
Subjects: LCSH: Gastrointestinal system—Juvenile literature. | Stomach—Microbiology—Juvenile literature. | Intestines—Microbiology—Juvenile literature.
Classification: LCC QP151 .D93 2020 (print) | LCC QP151 (ebook) | DDC 612.3/2—dc23

LC record available at https://lccn.loc.gov/2019049985
LC ebook record available at https://lccn.loc.gov/2019049986

Manufactured in the United States of America
1-46941-47815-4/3/2020

MASHA D'YANS

GARDEN IN YOUR BELLY

MEET THE MICROBES IN YOUR GUT

Millbrook Press • Minneapolis

Inside you flows a great river
with many folds and turns.

If you stretched this river into a straight line, it would be ten times as tall as you are! The river is your intestines— it nourishes a garden in your belly full of life and wonder called the microbiome.

This garden is **SO** small you can't see it unless you have a big microscope. But it's **SO** big that if you lined up all its tiny living microorganisms end to end, they would reach the moon.

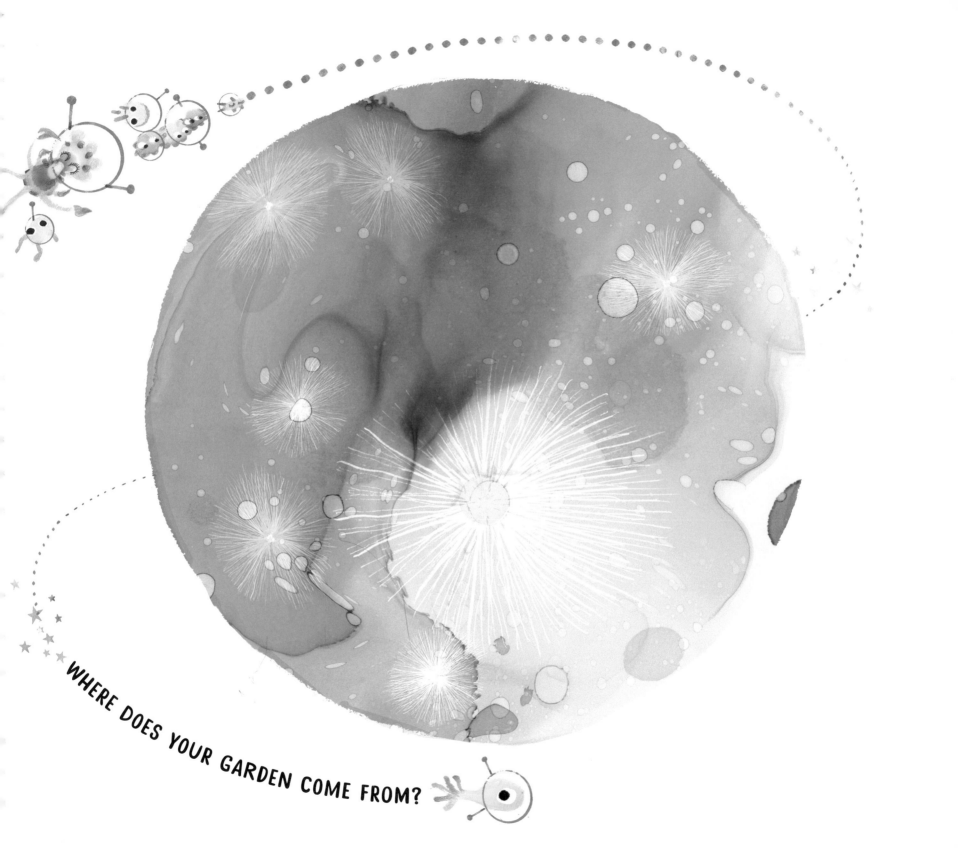

WHERE DOES YOUR GARDEN COME FROM?

You got the first seeds when you were born.
You collect more microbial sprouts by
breathing, touching, eating, and playing.

You get new microbes from your dog, from your best friend, from the ground underfoot, from food, and even from this book!

But no one on Earth has a garden exactly like yours.

Blooming of course . . . and making you **YOU!**

Your microorganisms come in many forms. Some are simple. Some are fancy. Some are friendly, and some are not.

Some kinds have existed for a million years!

Most microorganisms help your body do things it cannot do by itself. They protect **YOU** and the river every minute they're awake.

YES, WE SLEEP TOO!

As food passes through the river, each kind of critter has a different job to do.

The more variety your garden has, the better!

Your microbes harvest what they need to create energy and to fight germs. They also grow more microbes like themselves.

FROM YOU!

Your garden microorganisms put out fires and take the garbage out. Sometimes they have adventures and strange encounters.

They can even influence your thoughts and feelings.

Some of your microbes are connected to nervousness. They can make you feel like a restless butterfly.

Other critters are laid back, making you feel like a lotus floating on a pond.

Your microorganisms send you messages by adding froggy gurgles to the river when they want fertilizer to help them grow strong. They can make a beastly growl when you feed them something they don't like.

BUT CAN YOU TALK TO THEM?

You can't talk to them directly. But when you're playing outside, breathing fresh air, and drinking lots of water, the microbes know, and they're happy.

Doing these things is like
sending care packages down
the river to keep them strong.

After all, every
garden needs
attention and love.

If your garden critters get too hungry because you forgot to send healthy food, they get weak. Then the bad microbes can move into the garden like weeds. Bad microbes produce toxins that get in the river.

Your garden doesn't like pollution.

In the river, in the air, anywhere.

Pollution makes the garden weak,
which means the weeds can move in
and overpower your protectors.

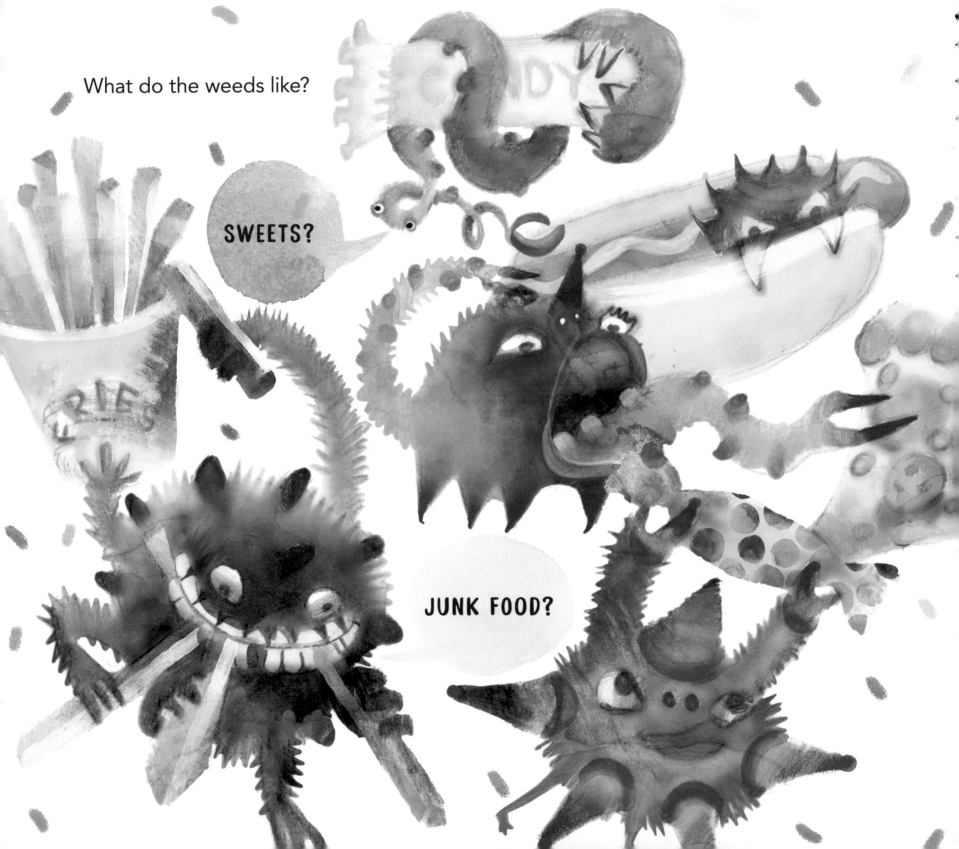

Just as the good guys can talk to you, the bad guys can too. They don't mind sending you messages to control your brain. If you eat only junk food, the next thing you know, **YOU** don't care for veggies and fruits or jumping and moving. You might even get sick. That's when it's time to grow back your protectors.

How do you grow your protectors and take care of them?

FEED THEM!

Take good care of your garden, and it will always have your back.

WHAT IS THE MICROBIOME?

A microbiome includes all the microorganisms living in a particular environment. The microorganisms living in and on the human body are one of the best examples of a microbiome. At this moment, 2 to 6 pounds (1 to 3 kg) of microbes are living in and on you. You're home to trillions of microorganisms, which are collectively known as the microbiome.

THERE ARE OVER 1,000 SPECIES OF MICROBIOTA ON THE SKIN, WHICH INCLUDE BACTERIA, VIRUSES, PROTOZOA, AND FUNGI.

THERE ARE OVER 700 SPECIES OF MICROBIOTA IN THE MOUTH, THROAT, AND LUNGS.

Your gut microbiome is constantly changing. At first, it is impacted by your parents, but it changes with every breath you take, every food you eat, and every person you meet. Your microbiome works best when there are lots of different kinds of microorganisms, bacteria, and microbes working together. The more diverse your microbiome, the stronger it is!

Scientists say that each microbiome needs different types of microorganisms to be healthy. There is no one microorganism that is the best to have in your microbiome. However, scientists have found that people with an abundance of Bacteroidetes and Firmicutes bacteria in their guts have the healthiest microbiomes. They may be part of what scientists call the functional core of the gut microbiome.

THE HUMAN GUT CONTAINS MORE THAN 100 TRILLION MICROORGANISMS AND IS CONSIDERED ONE OF THE MOST DENSELY POPULATED MICROBIAL HABITATS KNOWN ON EARTH.

GLOSSARY

FERTILIZER: a nutrient-rich substance that helps plants grow

HARVEST: to gather like a crop

INTESTINES: a part of the digestive system where nutrients and water are absorbed

MICROBIAL: relating to a microorganism or microbe

MICROBIOME: a community of microorganisms that live in a specific place, such as your body

MICROBIOTA: the microorganisms of a specific site or environment

MICROORGANISM: an organism of microscopic size, or microbe

MICROSCOPE: a device that uses lenses to allow people to see very small things in a magnified image

MICROSCOPIC: able to be seen only through a microscope: very small

NOURISH: to support growth and development

AMAZING GUT FACTS

A healthy microbiome can help fight off diseases and illness. Scientists are currently investigating how to treat diseases by treating the gut microbiome.

This microbiome acts as its own "brain." Unlike the rest of your body, your gut's not waiting for your head to tell it what to do. Why would it, when there are more than 100 million brain cells in your gut!

Food really affects your mood. Each thing you eat nourishes different microorganisms that make you feel one way or another.

There's one big nerve running from your gut to your head. And 90 percent of its fibers carry information from the gut to the brain, rather than the other way around. The brain interprets gut signals as emotions. So you really should trust your gut.

Your gut has its own nervous system too.

Your gut is your best friend in fighting germs. It works hard to help you get over what makes you sick by killing and expelling bad bacteria.

Did you know your microbiome makes you "gutsy"? Scientists are finding that your microorganisms can make you brave or timid depending on which ones you have more of.

Your microbiome is as unique as your fingerprints!

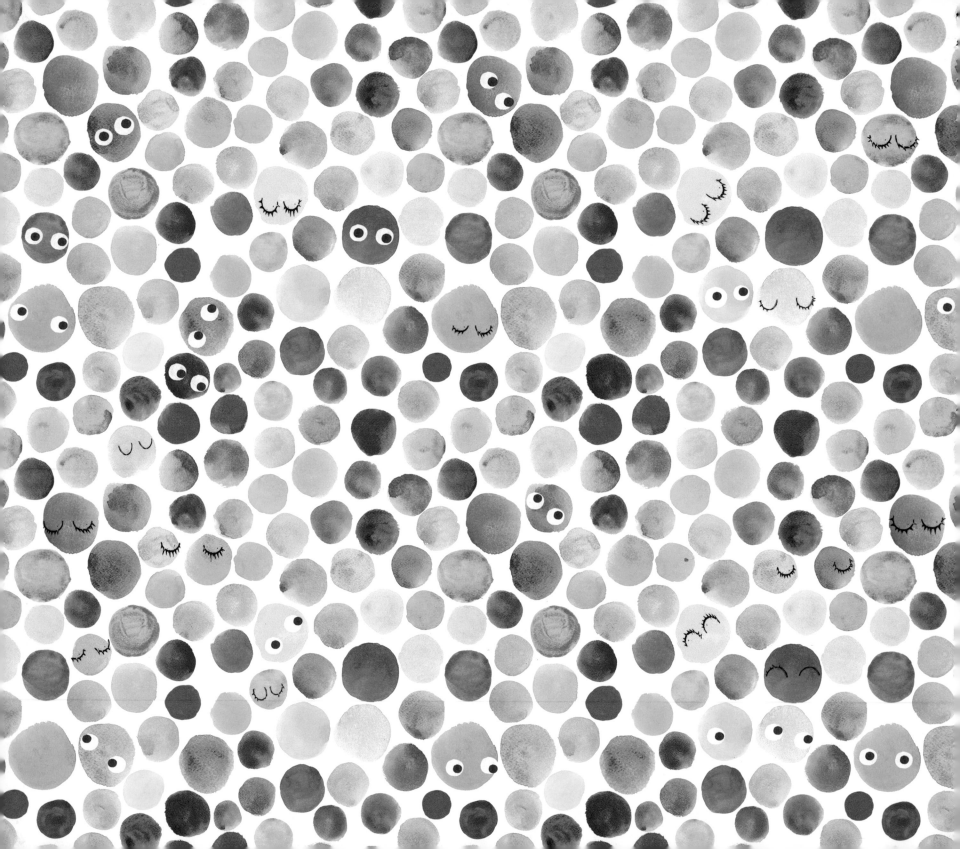